Table of Contents

Avalon Quickstep 6
The Baltimore 6
Bean Walker's Mile 7
Big-Eared Mule 7
Birdie 8
Black Jack Grove 8
Boggy Road to Texas 9
Bonaparte Crossing the Rhine 9
Bonaparte's March (A) 10
Bonaparte's March (B) 10
Bon Ton Schottische 10
British Field Marshal at New Orleans 11
Candy Girl (A) 11
Candy Girl (B) 12
Chinquapin 12
Cluck Old Hen (A) 12
Cluck Old Hen (B) 13
Coleman's March 13
Eli Greene's Cakewalk 13
Evening Pleasures Schottische 14
Evening Shade 14
Faded Love 15
Farewell Trion 16
The Fireman's Dance Cotillion 16
Forty Drops (A) 17
Forty Drops (B) 18
Fourteen Days in Georgia 18
The Glory in the Meeting House 19
Haning's Farewell 19
Hannah at the Springhouse 20
Happy Boy Schottische 20
Hard Road to Travel 20
Hawks and Eagles 21
In Come a Little Bee 21
Indian Ate the Woodchuck 21
Jan's Tune 22
John Brown's March 22
Just from the Mountain 22
Kanawha March 23
Kansas City Kitty 23

Lady Hamilton (A) 24
Lady Hamilton (B) 24
Leake County Two-Step 25
Let's Hunt the Horses 25
Limerock 26
Little Billy Wilson 27
Little Rose 27
Little Stream of Whiskey 28
Lowery's Quadrille 28
Maple Sugar 29
Marilla's Lesson 29
Martha Won't You Have
Some Good Old Cider 30
McKinley's March 30
Military Schottische 31
Monroe County Quickstep 31
Muddy Creek 32
My Little Home in West Virginia 32
Old Bob 33
The Old Ark's A-Movin' 33
Old Red 34
Onion Tops and Turnip Greens 34
Ora Lee 35
Pointe-Au-Pic 35
Pretty Little Dog 36
Pretty Little Indian (A) 36
Pretty Little Indian (B) 37
Redwing 37
Rose in the Mountain 38
Round the Horn 39
Rufus Rastus 39
Rutland's Reel 40
Sales Tax Doddle 41
Sally in the Garden 2 41
Sambo 42
Say Old Man,
Can You Play the Fidlle? (A) 42
Say Old Man,
Can You Play the Fiddle? (B) 43
Seneca Square Dance 44
Seven Come Eleven 44

Shady Grove 45
Shag Poke 45
Silver Bells 46
Sixteen Days in Georgia (B) 46
Sixteen Days in Georgia (A) 47
Sleep Lulu 48
Sleepy Lou 49
Snow Deer 49
Spanish Two-Step 50
Spring Creek Gal 51
Still on the Hill 52
Sugar Tree Stomp 53
Sweet Bunch of Daisies (A) 54
Swing Your Partner 54
Tennessee Mountain Fox Chase 55
Texas Quickstep 55
That Brownish Gal (A) 56
That Brownish Gal (B) 57
Three-in-One Two-Step 58
Tie Your Dog, Sally Gal 60
Train on the Island 60
Trot Along (My Honey) 61
Twinkle Little Star I 62
Twinkle Little Star 2 63
Two Friends Quadrille 64
Two White Nickels 64
Walking in My Sleep (A) 65
Walking in My sleep (B) 65
Washington Quadrille 66
Weavily Wheat 66
When the Leaves Begin to Turn Brown 66
Whistling Rufus 67
Wild Goose Crossing the Ocean 68
Wild Hog in the Woods 2 68
Wild Rose of the Mountain 69
Wink the Other Eye 69
The World Turned Upside Down 70
Wyzee Hamilton Special 70
Yew Piney Mountain (A) 71
Yew Piney Mountain (B) 71

Introduction

This is the last of five smaller books that reprint almost all of the music in *Volume Two* of *The Phillips Collection of Traditional American Fiddle Tunes*. It consists of a grab bag of tune styles that don't fit the categories of the four other books in this series (*Favorite American Rags & Blues for Fiddle, Favorite American Polkas & Jigs for Fiddle, Favorite American Hornpipes for Fiddle,* and *Favorite American Waltzes for Fiddle*.)

This compilation is not meant to teach how to fiddle, but to serve as a reference to the fiddler's repertoire.

To keep the books within a reasonable size, I have limited myself to mostly public domain tunes played in one of the several standard, but ill-defined geographic styles of the United States; New England, Southeastern and Bluegrass, Midwestern, and Southwestern. I have omitted what might be loosely called "ethnic" styles.

This music was learned from recordings, fiddle contests, jam sessions, dances, and meetings with individual fiddlers. I would like to thank Danny Gardella, Matt Glaser, Bill Christopherson, Kenny Kosek, Stuart Williams, Ruthie Dornfeld, Becky Miller, Paul Elliot, Tim O'Brien, Kerry Blech, Armin Barnett, Gere Canote, John Hartford, Tony Marcus, Ray Bierl, and Pete Sutherland for generously sharing their time.

I experienced extensive soul searching when considering bowing. Slur patterns contribute mightily to a player's style, but even the repetition of a selection is often bowed differently. In addition, it is virtually impossible to transcribe phrasing from a raucous old string band recording with complete accuracy. Therefore I have tried to capture at least the bowings most critical to a tune's interpretation. A novice fiddler will be able to learn a lot about the parameters within which players define good or "authentic" playing. I think it is essential that players not familiar with all manner of regional styles at least begin with the given notation.

All of these versions are taken directly from the playing of well-established fiddlers. The name in parentheses following the title identifies the chief source of the setting. Those with two names are based either on two recordings, or less often, when the chosen version used two fiddlers. If the music was taken from a commercial recording on which the fiddler was not identified, the name of the artist credited on the label is given after the fiddler's name.

Tunes with no indicated source were either based on my own arrangement, or had too many influences to be untangled.

Different versions of the same tune are notated by capital letters in parentheses, following the title. When two completely different melodies have the same title, they are notated by number.

Though I have tried to choose interesting settings for each tune, it is not my hope that any become the standard, just because they are in a book. The same applies to the suggested chord accompaniment. There are many interpretations that sound fine.

For a more in-depth introduction to *The Phillips Collection*, please see the introduction to *Volume One* of the series; *Hoedowns, Breakdowns and Reels*.

Stacy Phillips

Mel Bay Presents
Favorite American Listening Pieces, Two-Steps & Marches

for Fiddle
By Stacy Phillips

1 2 3 4 5 6 7 8 9 0

© 2008 BY MEL BAY PUBLICATIONS, INC., PACIFIC, MO 63069.
ALL RIGHTS RESERVED. INTERNATIONAL COPYRIGHT SECURED. B.M.I. MADE AND PRINTED IN U.S.A.
No part of this publication may be reproduced in whole or in part, or stored in a retrieval system, or transmitted in any form
or by any means, electronic, mechanical, photocopy, recording, or otherwise, without written permission of the publisher.

Visit us on the Web at www.melbay.com — E-mail us at email@melbay.com

DISCOGRAPHY

For recordings of the fiddlers in this book, consult:

    County Sales
    PO Box 191
    Floyd, VA 24091

and on line at:

    http://www.countysales.com/

Labels that record a lot of traditional fiddling include:

    Document
    County
    Rounder
    Missouri State Old Time Fiddlers Assoc.
    Voyager
    Rebel

Try web searches for these labels and individual fiddlers and tunes. Many current fiddlers distribute their own CDs.

Acknowledgements

I wish to recognize the generous help of the following for access to their record collections, and their willingness to share their knowledge of old-time fiddle tunes:

Armin Barnett, Ed and Geraldine Berbaum, Ray Bierl, Kerry Blech, Martha Burns, Gere Canote, Barbara Collins, Stephen Davis, Jim Day, Bill Dillof, Ruthie Dornfeld, Julie Durell, Paul Elliot, Frank Ferrel, Danny Gardella, Matt Glaser, Skip Gorman, Hank Haley, John Hartford, Matthew Hartz, Peggy Harvey, Penny Hauser, Dave Howard, Judy Hyman, Ron Kane, Shirley Koehler and Family, Kenny Kosek, Rich Levine, Larry MacBride, Tony Marcus, Mel Marshall, Peter Martin, Meghan Merker, Gary Lee Moore, Dale Morris, Tim O'Brien, Mosheh Savitsky, Susan Steingold, Pete Sutherland, Becky Tracey, Phil and Vivian Williams, Stuart Williams, and Tim Woodbridge.

Ruthie Dornfeld, Ellen Cohn and Dave Howard for yeoman editing.

TO ALL THE GREAT FIDDLERS WHOSE MUSIC CREATED THIS BOOK

Reading the Music Notation

Most of the notation is standard. I have included a few symbols which are particularly useful for fiddle music.

There are two notations for slides. In both cases, do not change fingering or bow direction.

1. **E1** Slide from the first note to the second. These glissandi are usually quick. Half-step slides with this notation sometimes begin a bit sharper than the indicated pitch; i.e., the slide may actually be a bit less than indicated.

2. **E2** This indicates a short (usually not more than a half-step), quick slide, either up or down. The pitch at the beginning of the slide has no duration.

When there are more than two sections in a piece, they are indicated by numbers—enclosed in rectangles. When there is an apostrophe after the section number (eg: 2'), it indicates an alternative version of that part.

The capital letters above the staff represent only one of many acceptable alternatives for chords. Occasional alternate or optional choices appear in parentheses.

The small numbers in parentheses that occasionally appear over the staff indicate fingering.

To minimize clutter, when a note drones through a whole measure or two (usually to an open string), I notate it a couple of times in characteristic places, and leave it to you to include as much of this effect as you wish.

AVALON QUICKSTEP (W. T. Namour)
a.k.a. "New Charleston No. 1"

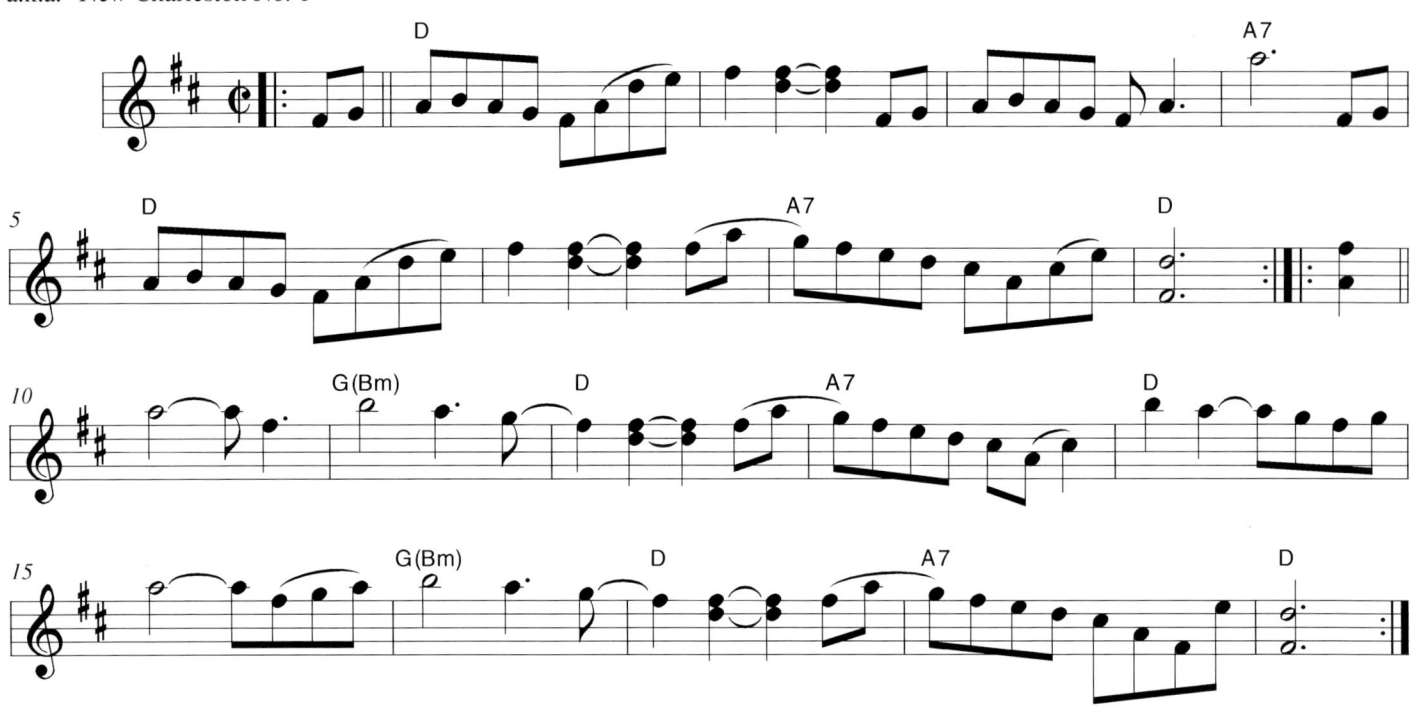

THE BALTIMORE (Lotus Dickey)

BEAN WALKER'S MILE (Lynn Smith)

The first section is the same as a tune titled Dominion Reel.

BIG-EARED MULE (John Salyer)

This is a breakdown that I found too late to place in *Volume One*. Add A string drones in Section One.
See the related "Flop Eared Mule" in *Volume One* of *The Phillips Collection of Traditional American Tunes*.

BIRDIE (Kenny Baker)

BLACK JACK GROVE (Walter McNew)

This version was unaccompanied. You can play an A major for the entire tune. McNew tends to blur the exact identity of C-naturals and sharps in section 2. This is a hoedown that was discovered too late to place in *Volume One* of *The Phillips Collection of Traditional American Tunes*.

BOGGY ROAD TO TEXAS (Hugh Farr)

BONAPARTE CROSSING THE RHINE (Tony Marcus)

Play only the fourth ending after "D.C. al Fine".

BONAPARTE'S MARCH (A) (Elmer Barton)

BONAPARTE'S MARCH (B) (Jehile Kirkhuff)

a.k.a. "Bonaparte Crossing the Rhine"

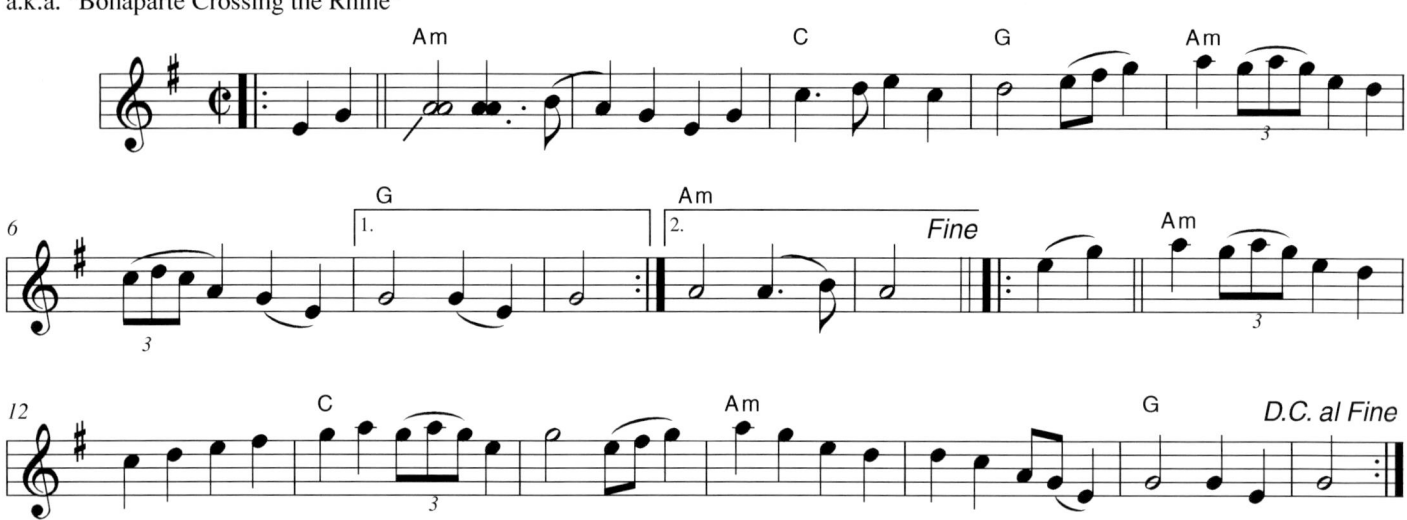

BON TON SCHOTTISCHE (Hugh Farr)

Play with a 6/8 feel.

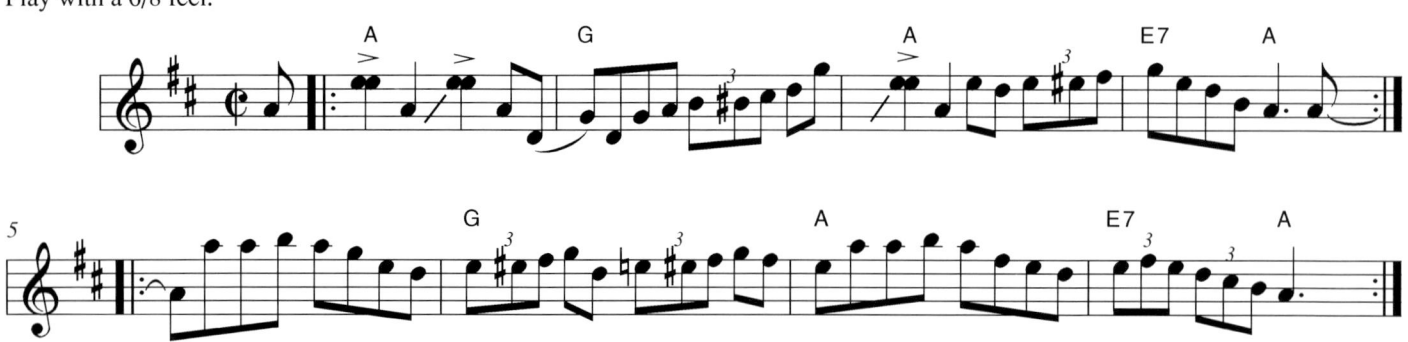

BRITISH FIELD MARSHAL AT NEW ORLEANS (Skip Gorman and Mark Jardine with the Deseret String Band)

Play slower than a breakdown.

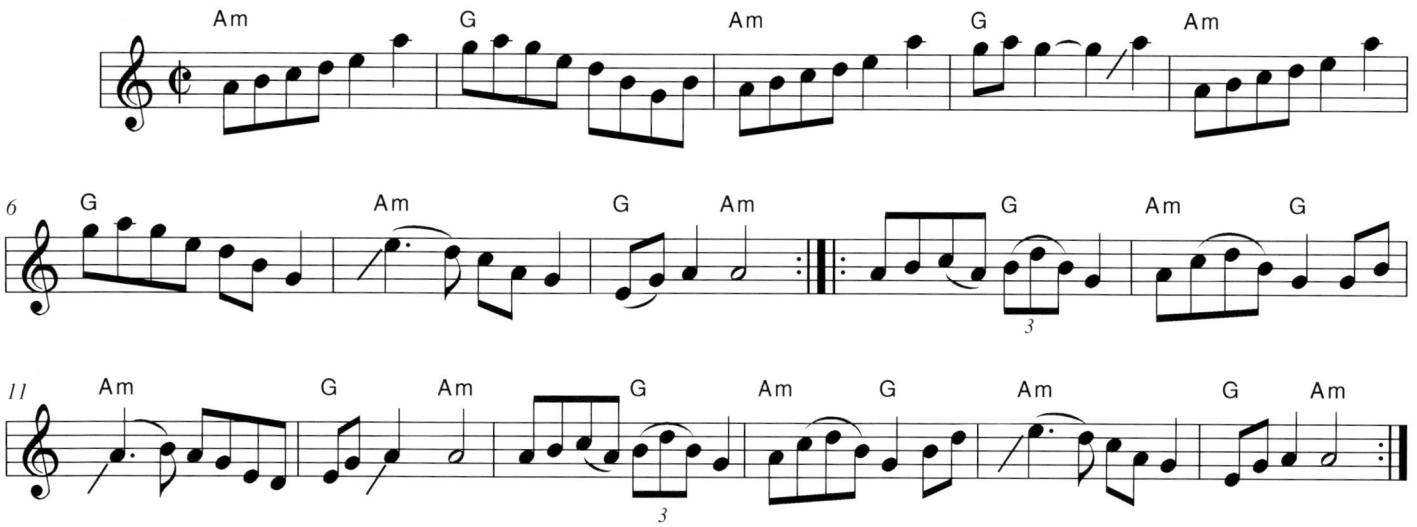

CANDY GIRL (A) (Bunt Stephens and Bruce Molsky)

This is often played in AEAE tuning. The repetitive eighth notes in section 1 are played slightly stacatto.

CANDY GIRL (B) (Kenny Barker with Bill Monroe)

CHINQUAPIN (Roscoe Parrish)

This version was unaccompanied.

CLUCK OLD HEN (A) (Ken Kosek)

Add A and E drones. In the second section, the "C" notes are sometimes played natural, with the parenthetical chords added.

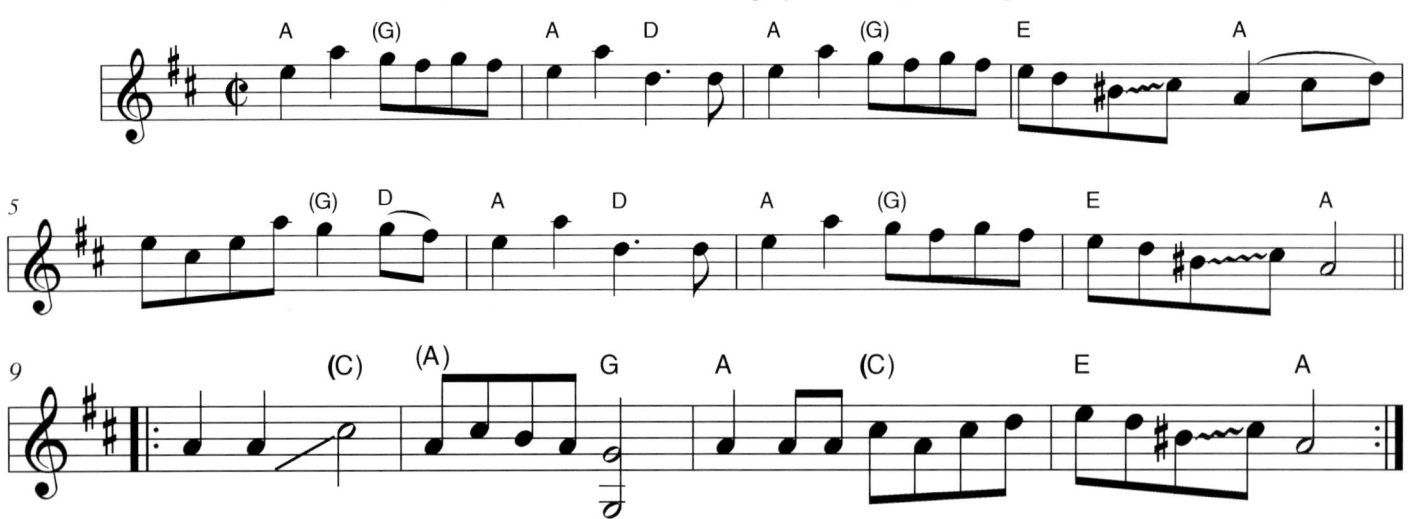

CLUCK OLD HEN (B) (Charlie Acuff)

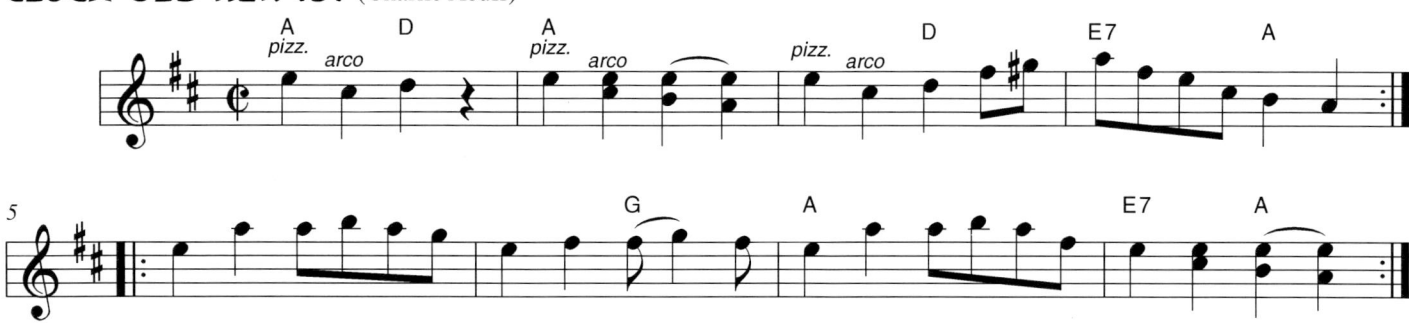

COLEMAN'S MARCH (Pete Sutherland)

This is usually played in DDAD tuning. Add A and D drones.

ELI GREENE'S CAKEWALK (Stuart Williams and Arlie Schaeffer)

EVENING PLEASURES SCHOTTISCHE (Tony Gilmore)

a.k.a. "Rustic Dance" and "Oh Dear Mother My Toes Are Sore."
Swing the 1/8 notes.

EVENING SHADE (Arthur Smith)

FADED LOVE by Bob Wills (Bob Wills, Johnny Gimble and Vassar Clements)

Words and Music by John Wills and Bob Wills. Copyright 1950, 51 by Bob Wills Music, Inc. Copyright renewed, assigned to Unichappell Music, Inc. (Rightsong Music, Publisher). International copyright secured. All rights reserved.

FAREWELL TRION (James Bryan with Bob Carlin)
Play slower than a hoedown. Play section 1 four times.

THE FIREMAN'S DANCE COTILLION (Jehile Kirkhuff)

FORTY DROPS (A) (Jere Canote)

This version was unaccompanied.

FORTY DROPS (B) (Kerry Blech)

FOURTEEN DAYS IN GEORGIA (Tommy Jackson)

See the related "Sixteen Days in Georgia."

THE GLORY IN THE MEETING HOUSE (Luther Strong)

Section 3 is played only once during Strong's version.

HANING'S FAREWELL (Kenny Kosek with Tony Trishcka)

This tune is too crooked to do anything but listen to. It helps to play a strong accent on the downbeat after the odd measures.

HANNAH AT THE SPRINGHOUSE (Melvin Wine)

HAPPY BOY SCHOTTISCHE (Stuart Williams)

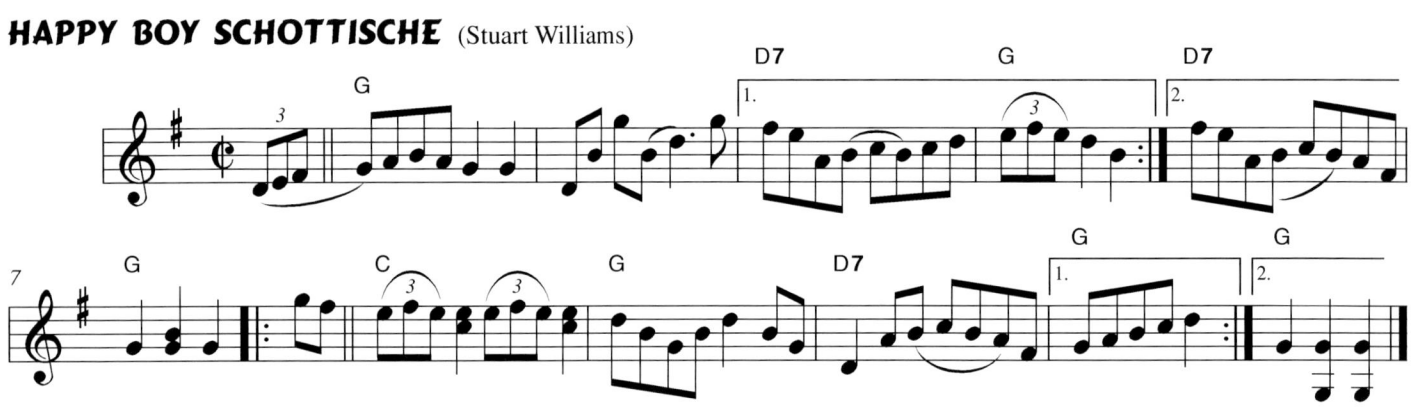

HARD ROAD TO TRAVEL (Jane Rothfield)

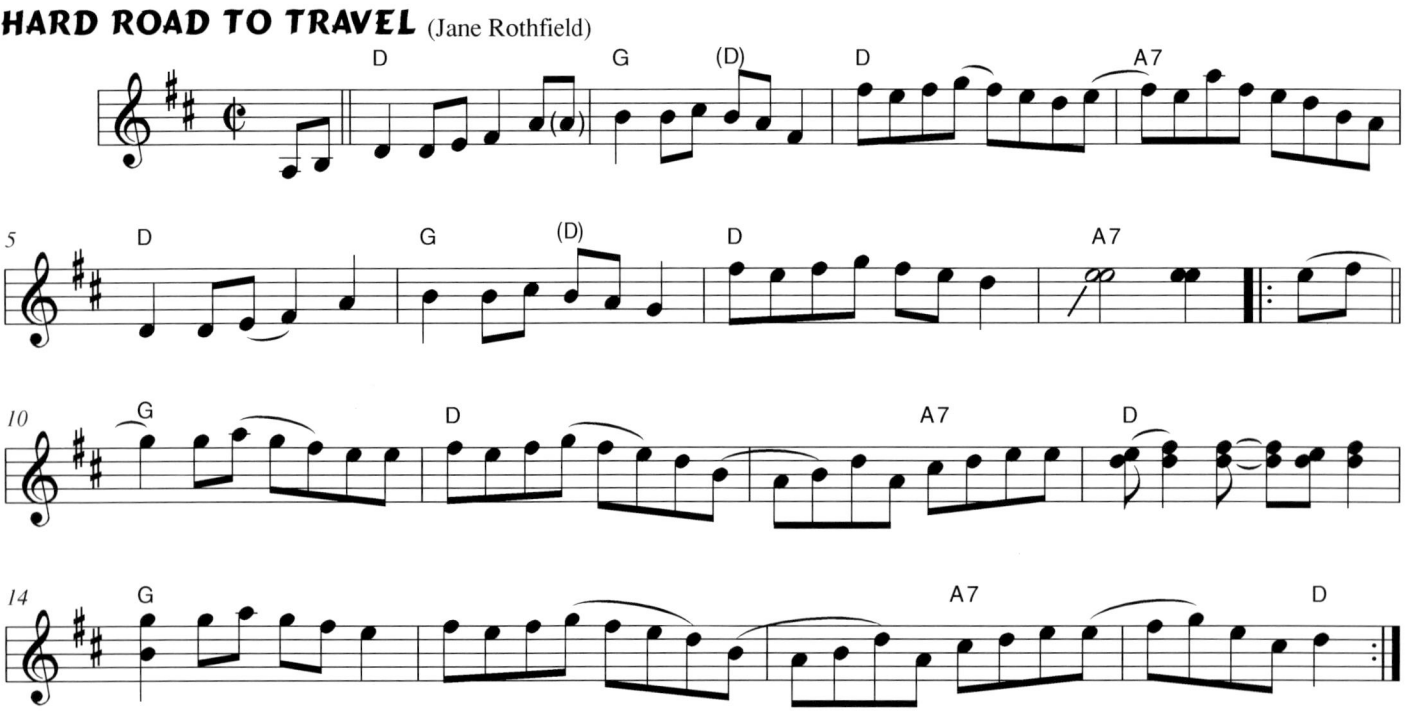

HAWKS AND EAGLES (Jane Rothfield)

The eighth notes must be swung to make this piece lively. This is a hoedown that was discovered too late to place in *Volume One* of *The Phillips Collection of Traditional American Tunes*.

IN COME A LITTLE BEE (Owen Chapman)

Play slower than a hoedown.

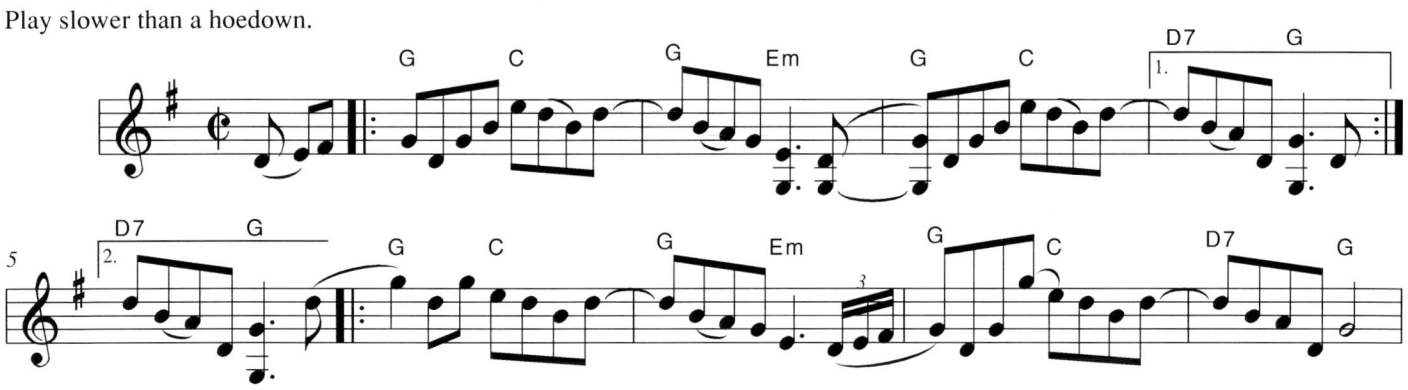

INDIAN ATE THE WOODCHUCK (John Salyer)

This is a breakdown that I found too late to place in *Volume One* of *The Phillips Collection of Traditional American Tunes*.

JAN'S TUNE (Brad Leftwich)

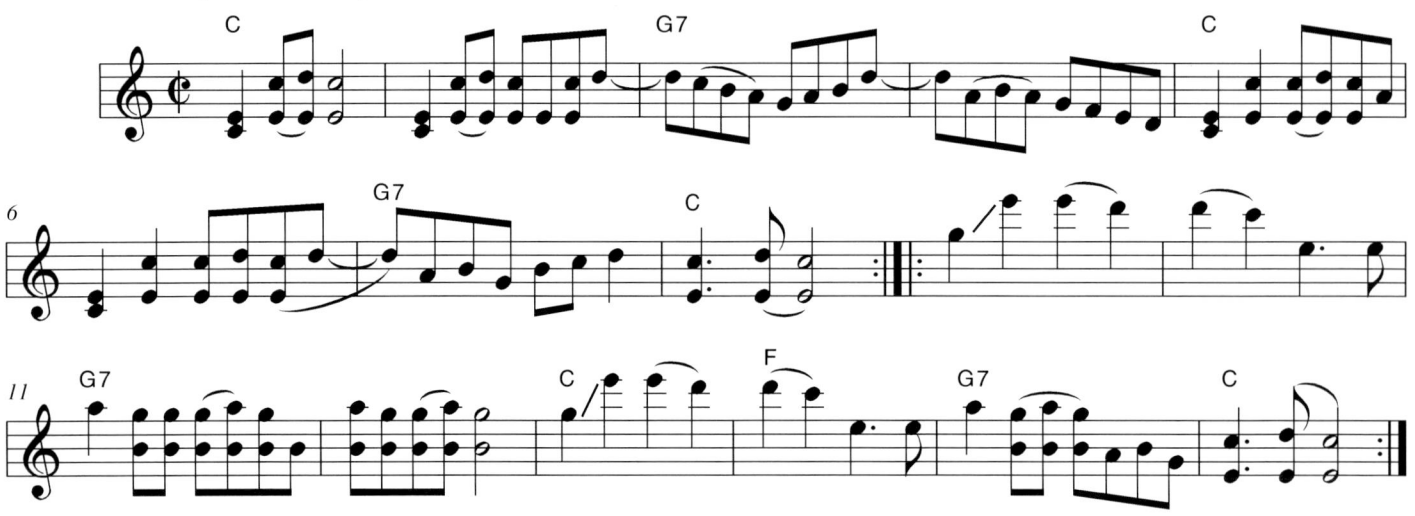

JOHN BROWN'S MARCH (Pete Sutherland)

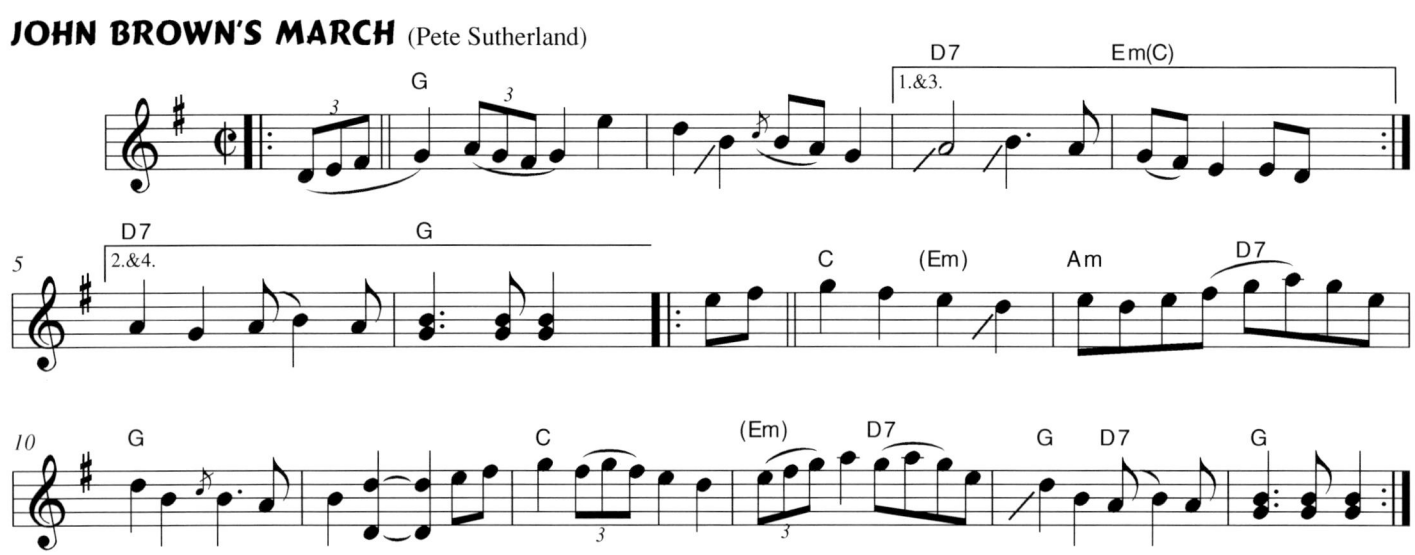

JUST FROM THE FOUNTAIN (Art Galbraith)

a.k.a. "Back to the Fountain"

KANAWHA MARCH (Clark Kessinger)

KANSAS CITY KITTY

The order of sections is 1-2-1 (one time). Play as a swing tune.

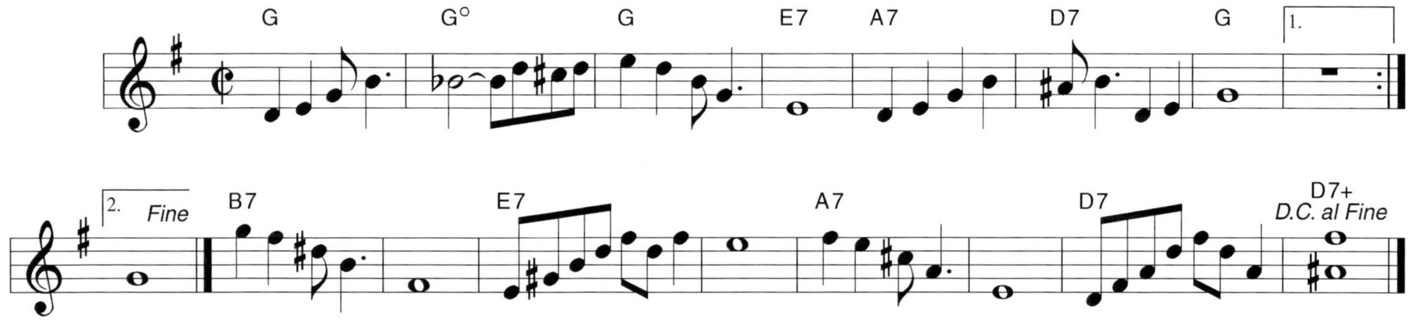

LADY HAMILTON (A) (Tony Marcus)

This version was unaccompanied.

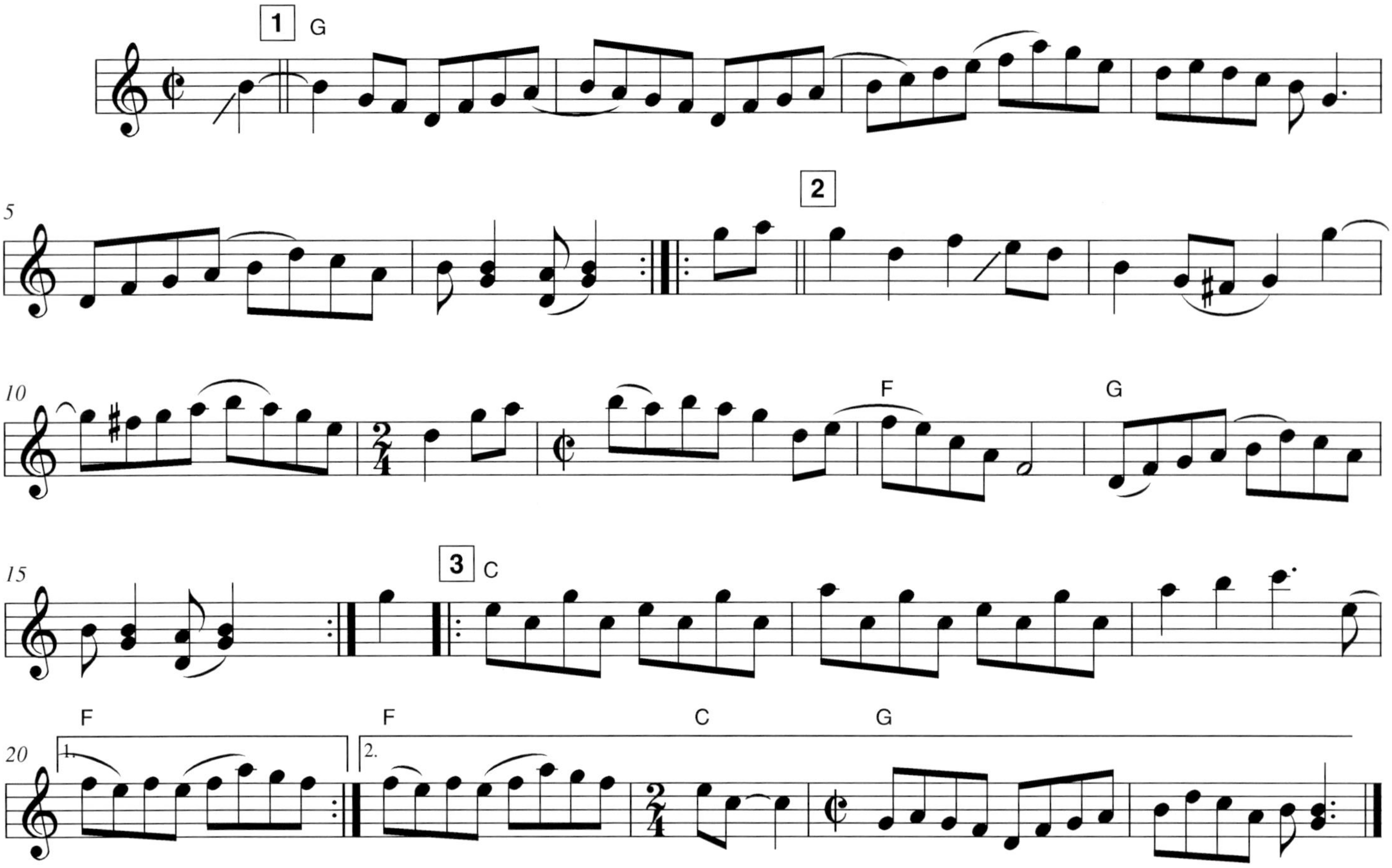

LADY HAMILTON (B) (Manco Snead)

The sharps in the parenthesis are played somewhere between sharp and natural. This version was unaccompanied.

LEAKE COUNTY TWO-STEP (Leslie Freeny with Freeny's Barn Dance Band)

Play this slower than hoedown tempo.

LET'S HUNT THE HORSES (Gerry Milnes)

Add A and E drones.

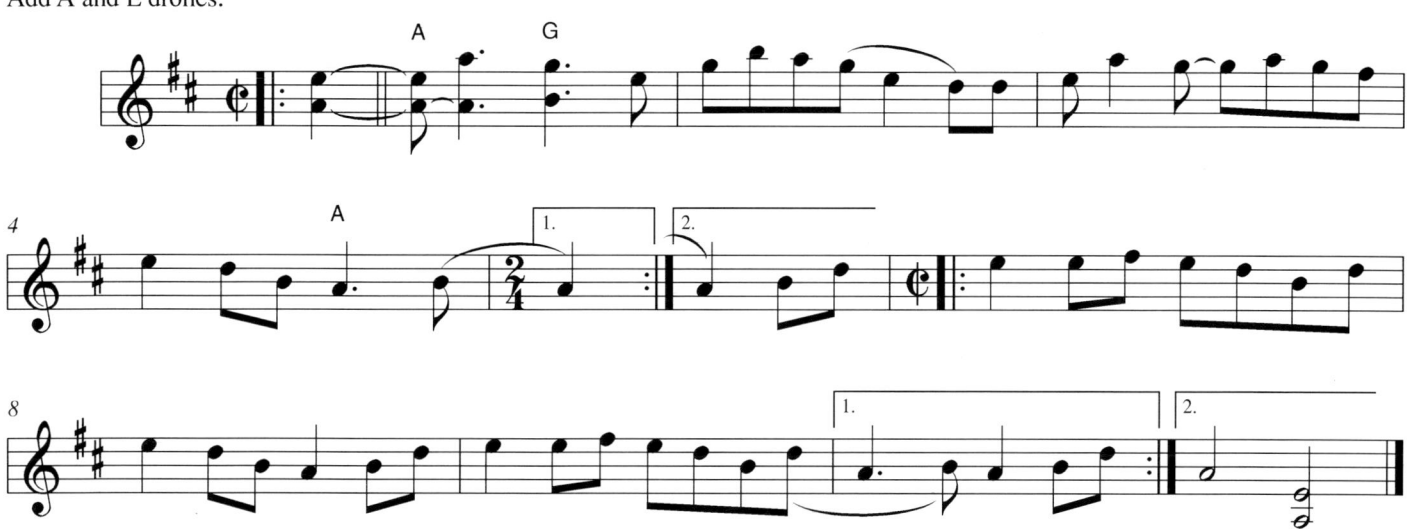

LIMEROCK (Byron Berline)

The order of sections is 1-2-1-3-1.

LITTLE BILLY WILSON (Jane Rothfield)

a.k.a. "Billy Wilson"
See "Ace of Spades" in *Volume One*. Add A and E drones. This is a hoedown that was discovered too late to place in *Volume One*.

LITTLE ROSE (Wilson Douglas)

This version was accompanied.

LITTLE STREAM OF WHISKEY (Doug Phillips)

The second section is attributed to Tommy Hunter.

LOWERY'S QUADRILLE (Armin Barnett)

MAPLE SUGAR (Pete Sutherland)

The order of the sections is 1-2-3-2. Add A and E drones.

MARILLA'S LESSON (Greg Canote)

The order of the sections is 1-2-1 (once through).

MARTHA WON'T YOU HAVE SOME GOOD OLD CIDER (Gaither Carlton)
Add D drones.

MCKINLEY'S MARCH (Kenny Baker and Howdy Forrester)

MILITARY SCHOTTISCHE

a.k.a. "Texas Schottische"
Swing the eighth notes. See the related "Helvetia Polka."

MONROE COUNTY QUICKSTEP (Leonard Rutherford)

Play each section four times.

MUDDY CREEK (Bruce Greene)

Play slower than a hoedown. This version was unaccompanied.

MY LITTLE HOME IN WEST VIRGINIA (Ellis Hall)

OLD BOB (Bruce Green)

Add D drones to the second section.

THE OLD ARK'S A-MOVIN' (Taylor Kimble)

a.k.a. "Keep the Ark A-Movin." Play slower than a hoedown.

OLD RED (Hoyt Ming)

ONION TOPS AND TURNIP GREENS (Bob Prater)

ORA LEE (James Bryan with Bob Carlin)

Play slower than a hoedown. Add G and D drones.

POINTE-AU-PIC (Ruthie Dornfeld)

This tune is also played in the key of G.

PRETTY LITTLE DOG (Ruthie Dornfeld)

Play slower than a hoedown. Add A and E drones.

PRETTY LITTLE INDIAN (A) (Curly Ray Cline)

Play slower than a hoedown.

PRETTY LITTLE INDIAN (B) (Matt Glaser)

REDWING (by Kerry Mills)

ROSE IN THE MOUNTAIN (John Salyer)

ROUND THE HORN by Jay Ungar (Jay Ungar)

' Jay Ungar Used by Permission

RUFUS RASTUS (John Holloway with the Mississippi Possum Hunters)

RUTLAND'S REEL (Howard Forrester)

The order of sections is 1-2-3-2-4-5-4-2. Section 1 is from "Dar's Sugar in the Gourd."

SALES TAX TODDLE (Shelton Nations)

Nations plays the melodic phrases a different number of times with each repetition of the tune. Play the quarter notes in measure 18-26 on the staccato side.

SALLY IN THE GARDEN 2 (Ken Kosek)

I have heard the Am and G chords substituted by A and E chords, respectively. Add E drones. "Sally in the Garden 1" is in *Volume One* of *The Phillips Collection of Traditional American Tunes*.

SAMBO (Kerry Blech)
This version was unaccompanied.

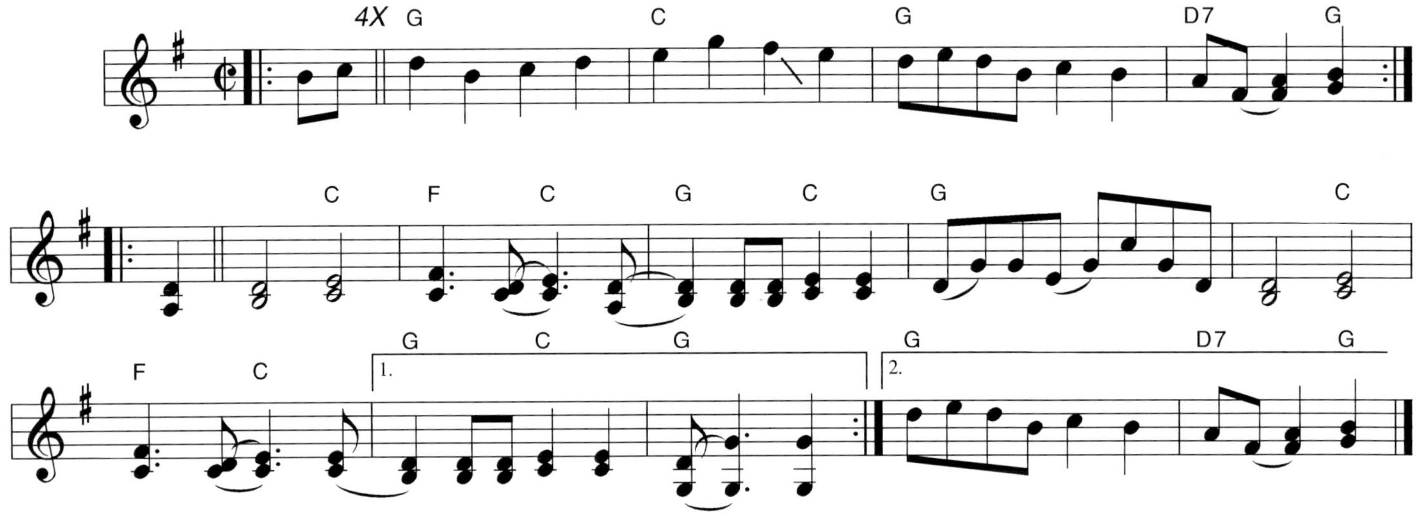

SAY OLD MAN, CAN YOU PLAY THE FIDDLE? (A) (Howard Forrester)
a.k.a. "Lady's Fancy"
"Lady's Fancy 2" is an unrelated tune a.k.a. "Preacher's Favorite." This tune is sometimes played with the G string dropped to E and used as a drone. In the first section the C notes can be played sharp.

SAY OLD MAN, CAN YOU PLAY THE FIDDLE? (B) (Joey McKenzie)

Many of the G notes are between "pure" natural and sharp. Add fingered and open E drones to section 2. The guitar accompaniment to this way in a swing style, with some passing chords.

SENECA SQUARE DANCE (John Hartford)

a.k.a. "Georgia Boys," "Waiting for (or Runing From) the Federals," "Got a Little Home to Go To" and "The Higher Up the Monkey Climbs."
Add D drones to section 1.

SEVEN COME ELEVEN (Frankie McWhorter)

Add A and E drones.

SHADY GROVE (Armin Barnett and Oscar Wright)
This version was unaccompanied

SHAG POKE (Pat Conte)

SILVER BELLS (Johnny Gimble and Cliff Bruner)

This tune has also been recorded in G, C, and B♭. Sometimes there is no key change in the second section.

SIXTEEN DAYS IN GEORGIA (B) (Ruthie Dornfeld)

Add E-string drones to section 1.

SIXTEEN DAYS IN GEORGIA (A) (Clark Kessinger)

The placement of the 2/4 measures reflects the phrasing of this setting. Add E drones to section 1. See the related "Fourteen Days in Georgia."

SLEEPING LULU (Bob Potts and Walt Koken with The Highwoods String Band and Ruthie Dornfeld)

SLEEPY LOU (John Ashby)

SNOW DEER By Percy Wenrich

aka "My Pretty Snow Deer"

SPANISH TWO-STEP (Bob Wills)

SPRING CREEK GAL (James Bryan with Bob Carlin)

Add A drones.

STILL ON THE HILL (Howard Forrester)

a.k.a. "Sells Brothers Circus Rag"

SUGAR TREE STOMP (Kenny Baker)

SWEET BUNCH OF DAISIES (A) (Kenny Baker)

"Sweet Bunch of Daisies" (B) is in the Waltz volume of this series.

SWING YOUR PARTNER (Kirk Sutphin with the Hollow Rock String Band)

a.k.a. "Second John Henry"

TENNESSEE MOUNTAIN FOX CHASE (Kirk Sutphin with The Hollow Rock String Band)

TEXAS QUICKSTEP (Red Steeley and Kenny Baker)

a.k.a "Texas Gallop" and "Black Jack"
See the related "Rachel" and "Short's Addition" in *The Phillips Collection of Traditional American Fiddle Tunes - Volume 1.*

THAT BROWNSKIN GAL (A) (Bob Wills)

THAT BROWNSKIN GAL (B) (Alexander Robertson)
a.k.a. "There's a Brownskin Gal Down the Road"

THREE-IN-ONE TWO-STEP (Daniel Williams with the East Texas Serenaders)

The order of sections is (1-2-3) three times 1-4-5.

TIE YOUR DOG, SALLY GAL (Kerry Blech and Will Adams)
a.k.a. "Tight Your Dog..."

This is a breakdown learned too late to include in Volume One. This version was unaccompanied. Play both or neither of the parenthetical chords.

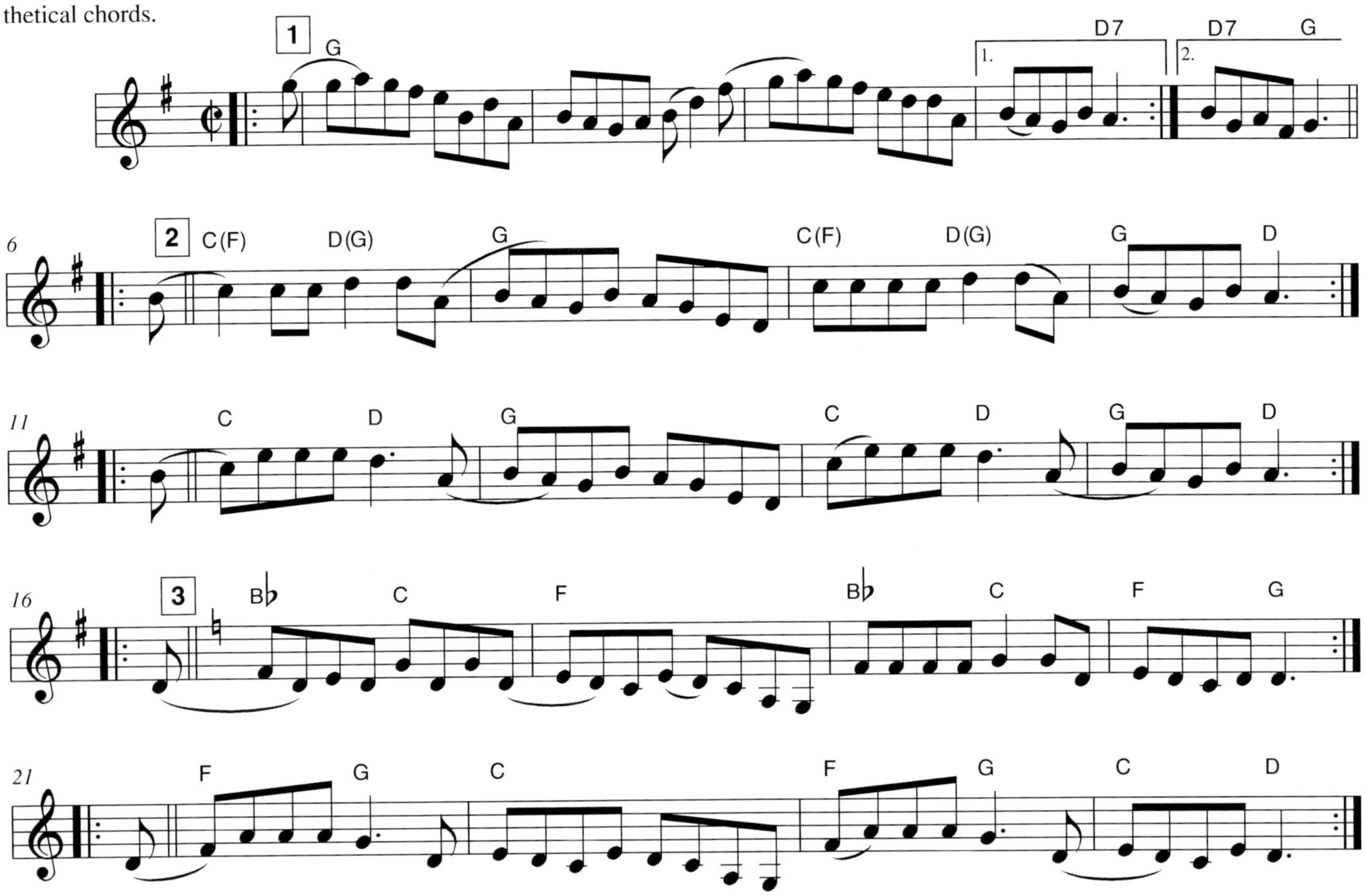

TRAIN ON THE ISLAND

Play slower than a hoedown. There is another tune with this name that is related to "June Apple". (See Volume One).

TROT ALONG (MY HONEY) (Howard Forrester)

TWINKLE LITTLE STAR I

TWINKLE LITTLE STAR 2 (Howard Forrester)
a.k.a "Little Star"

TWO FRIENDS QUADRILLE (Ron Kane with the Deseret String Band)

The order of sections is 1-2-3-4-3-4.

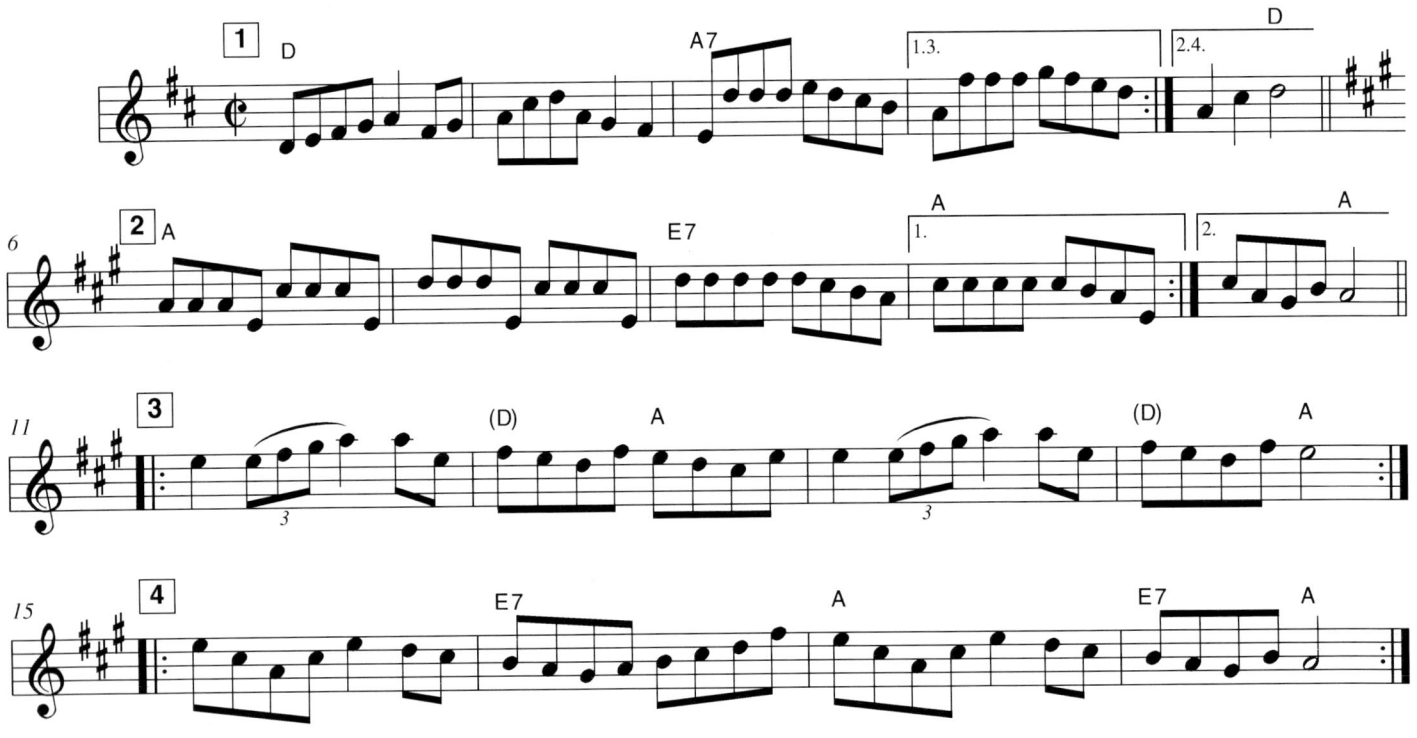

TWO WHITE NICKELS (Kerry Blech)

This is a breakdown learned too late to include in *Volume One* of *The Phillips Collection of Traditional American Tunes*. This version was unaccompanied.

WALKING IN MY SLEEP (A) (Dudley Spangler)

WALKING IN MY SLEEP (B) (Kenny Baker)

WASHINGTON QUADRILLE (Andy Palmer)

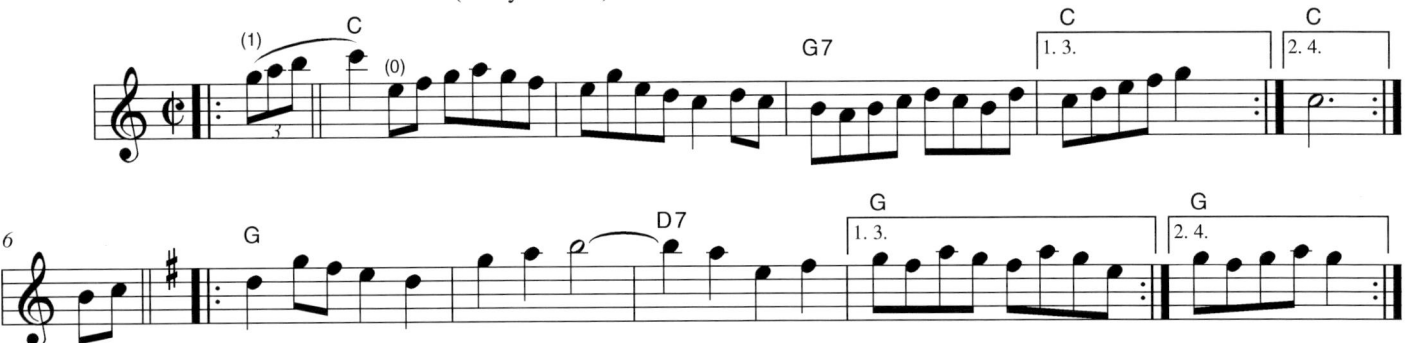

WEAVILY WHEAT (Kerry Blech)

This version was unaccompanied.

WHEN THE LEAVES BEGIN TO TURN BROWN (Tommy Jackson)

Add G and D drones to section 1 and A drones on the D chords in section 2.

WHISTLING RUFUS

The first sections is sometimes bowed as closely as possible to the bridge, resulting in a whistle-like tone.

WILD GOOSE CROSSING THE OCEAN (Alexander Robertson)

a.k.a. "Lost Goose" and "Wild Goose on the Ocean"
The harmonics, imitating a goose call, are fingered on the G string in first position. The note indicated as C sounds as a high G note.

WILD HOG IN THE WOODS 2 (Taylor Kimble)

Play this slower than a breakdown. The G note with the natural symbol in parentheses may be natural or sharp. This arrangement was adapted from one in GDGD tuning.

WILD ROSE OF THE MOUNTAIN (J.P. Fraley)

WINK THE OTHER EYE (Virgil Garett with Hack's String Band)

Play slower than a breakdown.

THE WORLD TURNED UPSIDE DOWN

WYZEE HAMILTON SPECIAL (Jere Canote)

a.k.a. "YZ Hamilton Special" and "Hamilton's Special Breakdown"

YEW PINEY MOUNTAIN (A) (French Carpenter)

Some of the G notes are sharpened a bit, and Cs notes are flatted. Add A drones to section 1 and E drones to section 2. Usually played in AEAE.

YEW PINEY MOUNTAIN (B) (Pete Sutherland)

This version was unaccompanied and is usually played in AEAE tuning.